Svetlana, Angel of Love

Youssef Khalim

Copyright © 2013 Youssef Khalim

All rights reserved.

ISBN: 978-0-9787810-4-0
ISBN-13: 978-0978781040

DEDICATION

To: Lori (The real or ideal soul mate: inspiration)

Tonya Tracy Khalim and

Runako Soyini Khalim, (my most beloved daughters)

Mother and Grandmother and Great-grandmother, (my most beloved maternal biological ancestors, and spiritual antecedents)

M. A. Garvey (one of my 7 M's: my role models)

Youssef Khalim II; III (my most beloved sons)

Father and Grandfather and Great-grandfather, (my most beloved paternal biological ancestors, and spiritual antecedents)

To: The Forerunners and Reincarnation sources (beloved biological ancestors and spiritual antecedents), and

The Almighty (our Spiritual Father), from whence we come.

CONTENTS

	Acknowledgments	i
1	Introduction	1
2	My One Desire in Life	Pg 2
3	This Time	Pg 3
4	This October	Pg 4
5	You Have The Power	Pg 5
6	Angel of Love	Pg 6
7	When A Man Loves A Woman	Pg 7
8	I'm Falling In-Love With You	Pg 8
9	And Then He Made The Woman	Pg 9
10	My Love For You Is So Darn Strong	Pg 10
11	That Other Mind	Pg 12
12	And Then I Met You	Pg 13
13	Share My Soul	Pg 14
14	I Love You More and More Each Day	Pg 15
15	You Are A Great Fascination For Me	Pg 16
16	Did You Ever Wonder How Life Works?	Pg 17
17	What I Love About You	Pg 20
18	You Give My Life Direction	Pg 21
19	I Will Shower Your Body With Love	Pg 22
20	Does God Hate George W. Bush?	Pg 23

21	What's Up With The Jefferson/Jacob Thing?	Pg 29
22	What Time Is It? It's Harvest Time!	Pg 32
23	You Will Never Find A greater Love	Pg 33
24	The Guy Who Missed The Flight That Crashed!	Pg 35
25	You Are Perfect!	Pg 36
26	Yes, I Love You	Pg 38
27	I Love To See You Dance!	Pg 39
28	About The Author, And Other Books	Pg 40

ACKNOWLEDGMENTS

To: The Forerunners and Reincarnation sources (beloved biological ancestors and spiritual antecedents), and

The Almighty (our Spiritual Father), from whence we come.

1 INTRODUCTION

I was born September 18, 1984, in a small village, near Moscow, Russia. I am logical, rational, and intelligent. However, my friends say it is great fun to be around me because I sometimes joke around, and have a good sense of humor.

I became interested in modeling in Russia, and I intend to pursue it as one of my goals. I am 5'8" tall, and I weigh 135 pounds. I have blue eyes.

I have a law practice in Moscow. My dream, later, is to marry and have children.

Svetlana,
October 31, 2004

Svetlana, Angel of Love is the sixth in a series of eight books by Youssef Khalim, begun in 2002. Four were inspired by ladies encountered over- seas. Svetlana is one of the four overseas encounters.

I met Svetlana in the fall of 2004, over the Internet. I saw her photo on New-Dating.Com, and e-mailed her. Later, I was struck by her extraordinary beauty and lovely personality. I wrote down my feelings, thoughts, and moods as fast as I could. Svetlana is the motivation and inspiration for this book.

Sometimes it seemed that the book was writing itself, and I was only a channel, trying to keep up. First, came *This Time*. Then, the other selections followed rapidly, and the book was complete in about 25 days, working part time. Svetlana has the most gorgeous, and sexy body, and attractive and charismatic personality, and I have attempted to capture and reflect her awesome presence and personality in *Svetlana, Angel of Love*.

Now I present to you the exciting, electric, and exotic *Svetlana*. Enjoy.

Youssef Khalim,
10/31/04

2 MY ONE DESIRE IN LIFE

Is to please you,
Love you,
Please you,
Love you,
And satisfy my one
Desire in life.

3 THIS TIME

I am here this time,
To love you,

Satisfy you,
Give you pleasure,
Joy, and happiness,

Safeguard our home
& family,
Aid, support, assist you,

And love you more each day,
Until the end
Of time.

4 THIS OCTOBER

You make me feel
Like I'm in heat,

This October.

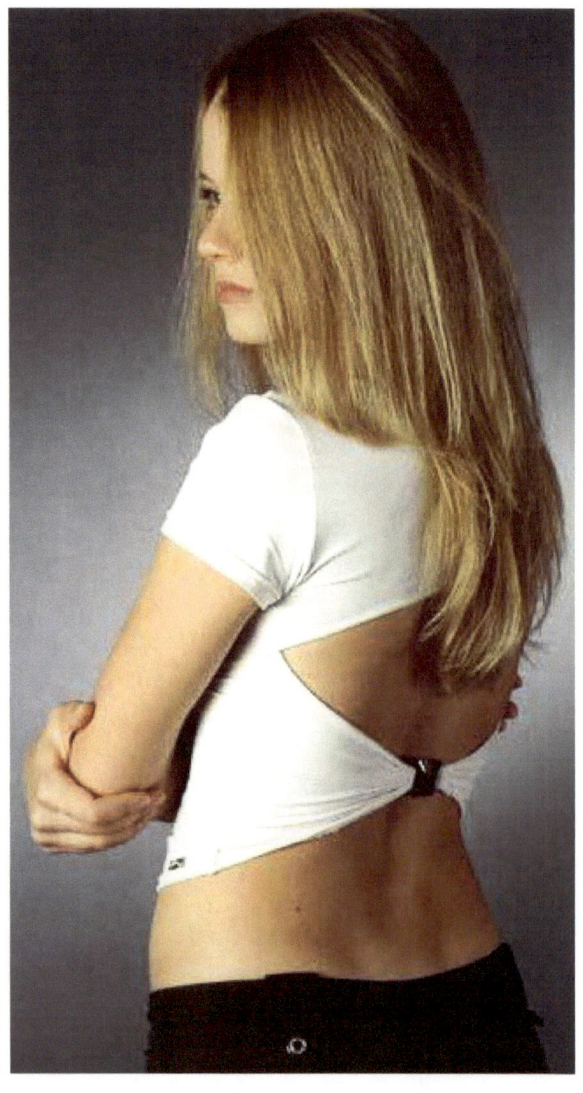

5 YOU HAVE THE POWER

You make me smile,
You give me joy,
Transform my soul,
You make me whole.

You touch my heart,
Make me a part,
Of you.

You have this awesome,
Awesome power.

You make me want to shower,
And shower
You back,

With love.

6 ANGEL OF LOVE

You are my lovely angel,
My gorgeous sweetheart,
My fantasy,
My dream come true,
My warmth,
Desire,
My ecstasy.

You are my lovely, lovely angel,
My heaven on earth,
My beautiful, sexy,
Fantastic,
Angel Of Love.

7 WHEN A MAN LOVES A WOMAN

She's always on his mind.

She elevates him,
Energizes, motivates,
Inspires him,

Makes sweet poetry stir
Deep down in his soul.

She gives him wings to soar,
Expands his chest,
And gives the breath of life,
Quickens his mind,
And makes him fearless,
Peerless,

Because he has to protect
The treasure she just made.

8 I'M FALLING IN-LOVE WITH YOU

I can feel you entering into my soul.
The process, movement, I feel,
Right here in my chest,
Right here by the best, in me.

My heart is making room for you,
A special place,
A special space,
Right here beside,
The One and only One,
That you and I will ever hold on high,
Adore and worship, praise.

9 AND THEN HE MADE THE WOMAN

He finished making the man,
And then he said,
Let us make woman,
From man.
Let us make her the most beautiful creation
In all creation,

Different from the man,
Lovely, pretty, like a flower;
The face, the body,
Talk and walk will be unique.

And she will complement the man,
And each will seek and make the other whole,
Fulfilled, complete.

Therefore, I sought and found you.
And now, I need you,
Because He said it,
Someone is missing
In creation,
And then He made you,
Beautiful, sexy, gorgeous, delightful, and wonderful.

Because He said it, let us make woman the most beautiful
Creation in all creation,

Then,
He made you.

10 MY LOVE FOR YOU IS SO DARN STRONG

My love for you is so darn strong,
Now, love like this just can't be wrong.

I have to try to write a song
About you.

I've got to try to tell the world,
How wonderful you are.
You are the very brightest star,
To light my life.

You are so beautiful, so sweet,
You are so kind, it's kinda neat,

The way you turn it on, turns me on,
Ignites me body, mind, and soul.

You ease this life for me,
You please me.
You even make me rather bold.

You give exactly what I need.
So, I've just got to write this song.
Let someone sing,
We can't go wrong.

Let's tell how you complete my soul,
Fulfill me,
Make me whole,
And give exactly what I need.

I am so happy now, with you,
I'm giving you your props, your dues.

So thanks, My Love,
I owe you tons of gratitude.

And, thanks to all the universe.
Let me rehearse these words, and verse.

I love you, and thank you for this:
This joy, pleasure and bliss,
I get from loving you,
And loving you,

And loving you, some more each day.
Because you've got just what it takes.

There's something wonderful about you, Dear.
And all I want,
Is all of you, just everything.
My Sweet-thing,

'Cause you are very, very hot!
And you have got
More than a lot:

A love that is so
Doggone strong,

A love so great
It can't be wrong,

And makes me want
To write a song,
About you.

11 THAT OTHER MIND

I Love your mind, Sweetheart.

I love your logical, rational mind.
Your thinking, questioning, searching, researching mind
Reminds me of Hillary, Gwendolyn Brooks, Randi Rhodes, Soledad O'Brien, Krystal Ball, Alex Wagner, Joy Reid, Karen Finney, Rachel Maddow, and Susan Taylor.

I know that we can grow together,
Our minds in unity, assisting, supporting, elevating
Each other,

Back to that Other Mind.

12 AND THEN I MET YOU

I thought I had met

The most beautiful woman in the world,

And then I met you.

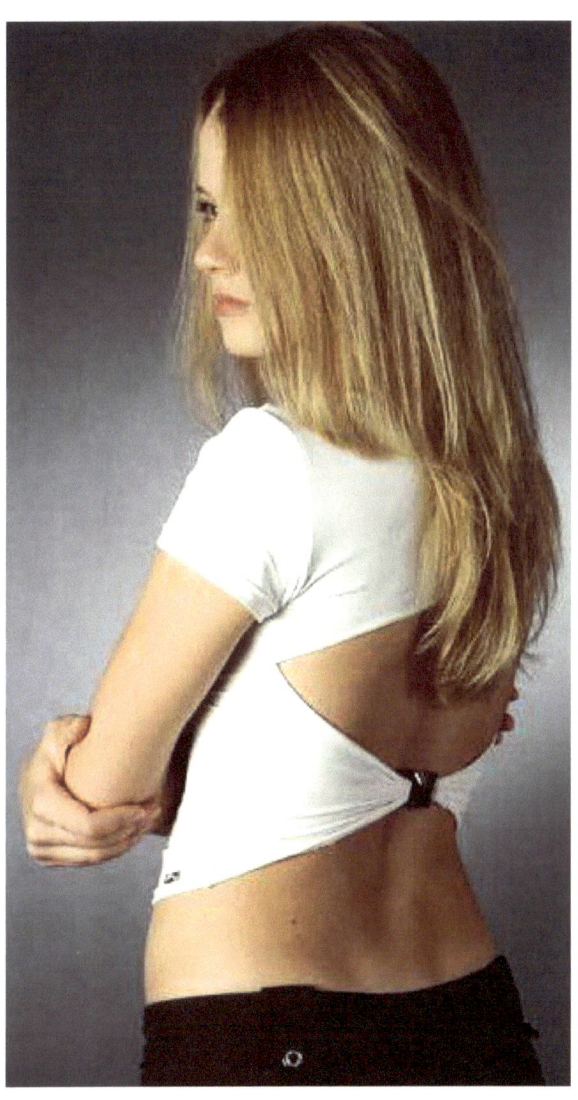

13 SHARE MY SOUL

It is an honor to know you,
A privilege to be with you,
Joy and heaven to love you,
And a blessing to have you,

In my life,
To share my soul,
And let me love you,
Be my wife.

14 I LOVE YOU MORE AND MORE EACH DAY

I want you more and more each day,
I need you more and more each day,

I have to have you,
Can't live without you,

Because I love you so.

I love you,
Need you,
Want you,
More and more each day.

15 YOU ARE A GREAT FASCINATION FOR ME

You are a great fascination for me,
And questions swim around in my head:
Why do I want you so?
And long for you so much,
And need to have you so?

Why do you look so much like heaven?
Why do I love you so?
Why do you look so wonderful?
So wonderful, terrific, fantastic?

Why do you melt my heart?
And make me want you
Forever and ever, and ever, and ever
And ever, forevermore.

16 DID YOU EVER WONDER HOW LIFE WORKS?

Did you know The Torah, Gospel, and Qur'an all say how life works,
And say, we live in the Eighth, and Last Empire?

Our "educated" class don't know this
'Cause they don't read those books,
Or the Upanishads, Bhagavad-Gita,
Or study Buddhist thought,
And they don't know
How to look for signs.

Life works and operates in cycles,
Like spring and summer,
Fall and winter, year after year, season after season.
And there is cause/effect, action/reaction,
Up and down, east and west: duality, many, many times.
And life on earth is just an instant in time.

Individual angels watch over us,
And we are born likewise, in seasons, and cycles,
Many, many times all over this planet
(And we visit other spheres).

And finally, in this Eighth, and Last Empire (called
Babylon, The Great), our souls are harvested,
Sorted, and the good and just reap appropriate rewards,
And bad ones get what they have sown,
For eight (8) is death, rebirth, regeneration, renewal.

And our country is part of the leadership
Of the Eighth Empire,
And rule this planet, along with
The European Union and NATO,
And everything created on the physical plane has a
Beginning and an end (called death or renewal).

Through yoga, meditation, and visions,
I saw these incredible things,
That confirm the Spiritual Theory of life,
As stated in the Spiritual Books.

I don't know *all* of what is not true, in the books,

But it truly looks,
Like I am Jacob.

And I confess,
The story of Jacob follows the pattern/cycles:
Third in the list of Patriarchs,
Following Abraham and Isaac,
Third president of the USA, in 1801.
Third of six children, born in 1743,
Third of six children, in the current cycle, with a "twin,"
Born in the third sign, Gemini.
And Thomas means twin,
As does Jacob, James, and Jimmy.

And when I fell asleep in 1826,
I fell asleep on July 4th, AS A TWIN,
With my brother, John Adams,
An incredible sign and miracle, for you.
And I confirmed this theory on August 4, 1999,
Through meditation, and as seen in vision,
Through the mercy of God.

And of greater importance to me,
I saw in awesome vision, on 5/2/2000,
That Prophet Muhammad *is* the reincarnation of Moses,
And this is perhaps,
The most important news I have to give.
And was confirmed likewise,
But in an awesome, awesome vision,
For the sands
Morphed, in the desert, into a face,

And in answer to my question, then and there:
"Is Prophet Muhammad the reincarnation of Moses?"
The winds stopped swirling, and the sands
Stood still.
The face said, "Of course!"

So, I am here this time to help prepare for Harvest,
And give my witness,
And say,
We are all Children of God, brothers, and sisters alike.
And God loves all of us,
And at our best, "We Are Love."

But the universe is cause/effect, action/reaction,
And it is just about Harvest Time, maybe within 8-years.

And The Books say Jacob is father to all mankind,
And likewise Jefferson, through the Declaration,
And the ideals. See how the patterns work?

So, now that I have found you,
Let us love each other, share and care,
And give our witness, forgiving others,
Receiving forgiveness, as an effect,

Remembering,
The universe is cause/effect, action/reaction,

And that is how life works.

17 WHAT I LOVE ABOUT YOU

The way you smile,
Your warm, sweet mouth,
Your gorgeous, heavenly chest,
The way you tilt your head to one side before you speak,
Your lovely voice,
The way you talk,

The way you move your body to the music,
The way you dance,
To hear you sing,
Your beautiful eyes,
The cozy, passionate way you hug me,
Your passionate kiss,
To touch your soft, warm skin,
The way you close your eyes, to feel and listen,
How wonderful it is to see you peacefully sleeping,

The way you walk,
Your divinely sculptured, and beautiful back,
Your curvy hips,
Your divinely beautiful face,
Your beautiful, sexy mouth,
The way you pout,
Your exotic, sensual smile,
Your clever mind,
Determination,
Character,
Charisma,
Personality,
The thought of you,
And your presence.

.

18 YOU GIVE MY LIFE DIRECTION

Focus, drive.
You energize me,
Anchor me,

So, I can tell the world
How much I thrive on loving you,
Listening to music with you,
Taking a walk with you,
Attending a concert together,
Massaging your shoulders,
Holding you in my arms,
And loving you.

Then telling the world that
Life is great.
God is Great,
And real,
In us,
And we, in Him.

A New Day's coming,
And all of us
Will love each other like we do,
Share and care,
Have a New Direction,

I will be a part of you,
And you a part of me,

And He will be in us,
And we in Him,
Anchored,
Among the people,
And blissfully headed,
In a New Direction.

19 I WILL SHOWER YOUR BODY WITH LOVE

Adore you,
Love you,
Need you,
Want you,
And love you,
Love you,
Love you,
Love you,
And love you,
Forevermore.

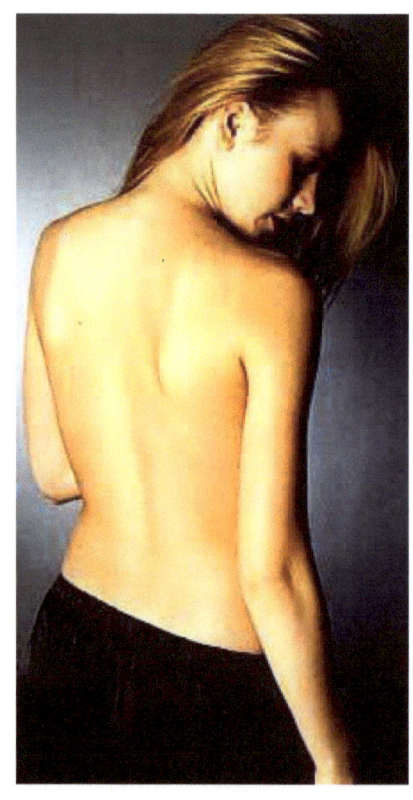

20 DOES GOD HATE GEORGE W. BUSH?

God is that force that brings you
Into this world,
And He takes you out.

He's life, and love.
And *levels of consciousness*.

He's action/reaction, cause/effect,
Cycles, patterns, and justice.

He's weather, nature, hurricanes, tornadoes,
And, believe me, He's everywhere.

Therefore they said, an eye for an eye,
Tooth for a tooth, and a life for a life.

And the Lord, our God is One,
And made the patterns of Ancient Israel,
The 42 Prophet Kings, Philosopher-Priests
Of Matthew, and of Luke.

Likewise, are the patterns in the USA.
For Jefferson, our third President, is Jacob,
Setting the patterns, fulfilling the prophecies,
And setting the boundaries, and ideals of
Our Republic,

    You see it:

1.	Abraham, Gen. 11:26	Like	George Washington, 1789
2.	Isaac, Gen. 21:2	Like	John Adams, 1797
3.	Jacob (Israel), Gen. 25:26	Is	Thomas Jefferson, 1801
4.	Judas, Gen. 29:35	Like	James Madison, 1809
5.	Phares, Gen. 46:12	Like	James Monroe, 1817
6.	Esrom, Gen. 46:12	Like	John Quincy Adams, 1825

7.	Aram, Ruth 4:19	Like	Andrew Jackson, 1829
8.	Aminadab, Num. 1:7	Like	Martin Van Buren, 1837
9.	Nasson, Num. 1:7	Like	William I. Harrison, 1841
10.	Salmon, Ruth 4:20	Like	John Tyler, 1841
11.	Booz, Ruth 4:21	Like	James K. Polk 1845
12.	Obed, Ruth 4:17	Like	Zachary Taylor, 1849
13.	Jesse, Ruth 4:22	Like	Millard Fillmore, 1850
14.	David, 1 Chron. 2:15	Like	Franklin Pierce, 1853
15.	Solomon, 2 Samuel 12:24	Like	James Buchanan, 1857
16.	Roboam, 1 Kings 11:43	Like	Abraham Lincoln, 1861
17.	Abia, 1 Kings 15:1	Like	Andrew Johnson, 1865
18.	Asa, 1 Kings 15:9	Like	Ulysses S. Grant, 1869
19.	Josaphat, 22:41	Like	Rutherford B. Hayes, 1877
20.	Joram, 2 Kings 8:16	Like	James A. Garfield, 1881
21.	Ozias, 2 Kings 8:25	Like	Chester A. Authur 1881
22.	Joatham, 2 Kings 15:32	Like	Grover Cleveland, 1885
23.	Achaz, 2 Kings 16:1	Like	Benjamin Harrison 1889
24.	Ezekias, 2 Kings 18:1	Like	Grover Cleveland, 1890
25.	Manasses, 2 Kings 21:1	Like	William McKinley, 1897
26.	Amon, 2 Kings 21:18	Like	Theodore Roosevelt, 1901
27.	Josias, 2 Kings 21:24	Like	William H. Taft, 1909
28.	Jechonias 1 Chron. 3:16	Like	Woodrow Wilson, 1913
29.	Salathiel, 1 Chron. 3:17	Like	Warren G. Harding, 1921
30.	Zorobabel, 1 Chron. 3:19	Like	Calvin Coolidge, 1923
31.	Abiud, (Matthew)	Like	Herbert C. Hoover, 1929
32.	Eliakim, (Matthew)	Like	F. D. Roosevelt, 1933
33.	Azor, (Matthew)	Like	Harry S. Truman, 1945
34.	Sadoc, (Matthew)	Like	Dwight D. Eisenhower,1953
35.	Achim, (Matthew)	Like	John F. Kennedy, 1961
36.	Elind, (Matthew)	Like	Lyndon B. Johnson, 1963
37.	Eleazar, (Matthew)	Like	Richard M. Nixon, 1969
38.	Matthan, (Matthew)	Like	Gerald R. Ford, 1974
39.	Jacob, (Matthew)	Like	Jimmy Carter, 1977
40.	Joseph, (Jesus' father)	Like	Ronald Wilson Reagan, 1981
41.	Jesus, (Matthew)	Like	George H. W. Bush, 1989
42.	Christ, (Matthew)	Like	William J. Clinton, 1993
43.	None; Dispensation over.	Like	George W. Bush, 2001
44.	None; Dispensation over.	Like	Barack Obama, 2009

Very often the comparisons show the very, or very opposite. Some of the comparisons are listed below:

1. Abraham, and George Washington moved away from their nations and started new nations. Washington was a warrior; Abraham fought against Chedorlaomer (Gen. 14:5).

3. Jacob (Israel) is the father, through his offspring, of the Hebrew nation and the West. Jefferson is the father of the ideals of the USA.

14. Franklin Pierce became the youngest President of his time. He hastened the Civil War by signing the Kansas-Nebraska Act of 1854. David was a young warrior, and the best in his character was the opposite of Pierce's.

15. Solomon was wise, and had about 1000 "wives." James Buchanan is considered one of the worst presidents because of his lack of judgment and moral courage, and the only bachelor President.

16. Abraham Lincoln saved the Union and is considered a moral individual. His counterpart, Roboam, presided over the breakup of the Jewish State into Judah, and Israel. Roboam was immoral.

28. Woodrow Wilson was a good man. His counterpart, Jechonias was a scoundrel.

30. Calvin Coolidge said the business of America is business. Salathiel, the counterpart said the business of Israel was justice and righteousness.

39. Jacob, of course is another word which means James, Jimmy, Israel; and it means "he who would provide service to his fellow man." So, Jimmy Carter works for "Habitat," an organization that provides services from man, to his fellow man.

40. Joseph (Jesus' "father") helped to prepare a channel that became the hope of humanity. The World is forever indebted to him. He went to Egypt to avoid death to his son. The counterpart, Ronald Reagan, presided over the USA becoming the world's biggest debtor nation.

Also, the national debt went from $1 trillion to 3 trillion. Reagan invaded tiny Grenada, and bullied other small nations. He also said things that had little or no resemblance to facts. MANY USA CITIZENS JUST LOVED Reagan!

41- 42. Jesus was oppressed and escaped to Egypt to save his young life. As the Christ, he made a way for many, to save many lives...

To tell the truth,	To be of service
To heal the sick	To feed the hungry
To give man hope	To lift the oppressed
To free the captives	To comfort the weary

To encourage those who fight against evil

To Lead Man Back To His Final Destination!

Bush, the counterpart, invaded Panama. He killed the children, and women, and men in his way. He murdered tens of thou- sands of children, women, and men in Iraq. The USA citizens loved it. Jesus the oppressed, Bush, the oppressor! Opposites!

During the time of Bill Clinton, the price of oil declined to about $10-11 per barrel. Surpluses appeared in the Federal Budget. The Internet and The Dot-Com bubble appeared. And some thought that the Clinton era prosperity signaled the end of regular economic cycles. And this reminds us of Jesus feeding the multitude of 5 thousand men, plus women and children, with 5 loaves and 2 fishes, and taking up, after everyone had eaten, 12 baskets full of fragments, that remained. (Matt. 14: 17-21). And the 4 thousand men, plus women and children, fed with 7 loaves, and "a few little fishes." "And they took up of the broken meat that was left 7 baskets full." (Matt. 15: 34-38). After Jesus left the scene, and after Steven was stoned, in 34 AD, the Covenant with Ancient Israel ended. And the dispensation (mission, torch) was given, in-turn to the Christians, and then to the Muslims.

And after Clinton, the Covenant with America ended, So,
The Supreme Court selected the next president,
George W. Bush,

And it's not that God hates Bush,
And the Bush Family,
But their evil is reflected back on them,
And the *real* evildoers
Receive what they have earned,
And you will know them by their fruit,
And *see* what they have earned.

For the universe is action/reaction, cause/effect,
Cycles, patterns, and justice.

And 911 happened,
Because the covenant expired,
And, just as ancient Israel failed to live up to
Its agreement,

So has America.

And 911 is a taste of America's future: war, insecurity, famine (recession), and lack of freedom.

But 911 should also be viewed as an overall, organic process,
Signaling the downfall of the leader of this era,
And the beginning of the Millennium.
On 911, there were the airplane attacks in New York, Washington, D.C., and Pennsylvania, plunging the USA into recession, fear, and the "War On Terror," and enabling The Patriot Act, Homeland Security, Threat Level Color Codes, and other such measures.

From March through October, 2001, there was an "official" recession-but today (on 10/6/03), many talk as if the USA is still in recession, in part, because of its "job- less recovery."

From about October 9, 2001, through about August, 2002, there was the case of the Anthrax letters in the USA, which killed 5 people and scared millions.

On November 12, 2001, there was the crash of Flight 587, an Airbus, in Queens, N.Y., that killed 260 people.

In October, 2001, the USA went to war against Afghanistan and Al Qaeda, and today, there are indications of an increasing resurgence of the Taliban and Al Qaeda.

In October, 2002, the DC area sniping began, resulting in the deaths of 10 people, and the terrorizing of millions.

In March, 2003, the USA began a preemptive war against Iraq, and it has evolved into a guerrilla war.

In 2000, there was the Florida elections fiasco, and the installation of George W. Bush to the presidency through the efforts of the US Supreme Court.

In 2003, there was the Texas Republican redistricting coup. And in California, there was the successful effort to recall Governor Gray Davis.

In the summer of 2004, 4 hurricanes hit Florida:

Charley, Frances, Ivan, and Jeanne.
And, you will know them by their fruit.
For in this era,
Bad things happen to bad people.
Now, note the pattern:
For, in the beginning,
It was George, John, Thomas (or twin),
And in this cycle, after the 42 legitimate ones,

It is George, then Barack Obama.

Will we get a third president, in this new cycle of patterns, or will Jacob, and others (symbolically) call-in the Harvest?

Will God, (actually), gather it in?
We *will* watch the "fruit."

21 WHAT'S UP WITH THE JEFFERSON-JACOB THING?

I think the most important thing
I can do,
In this lifetime,
Is to try to explain
How life works.

So, try this:
The Holy Books appear to be more valid
Than you thought,
Than I thought.

About me: I practiced yoga,
I learned to meditate,
Sometimes.

I studied the prophecies of Daniel,
Revelation, The Torah, and The Gospels.
I analyzed the Qur'an,
Studied all religions,
And I learned some things
About Hindus, Buddhists,
You name it.

I maintained maximum integrity
In all religious and spiritual matters,
For, who needs more confusion than we have?

So, let me say this:
This is really unbelievable, OK?

But, life is action/reaction, cause/effect,
Cycles, patterns, balance, harmony, and justice.

Night, day, summer, fall, winter, spring,
Cycles, can you see it?
All things created on earth come to an end.

We are all Children Of God,
Having consciousness in Him,
Living in Him,
For He is Life.

And life is love,
It is the joy of existing!

We are meant to hate injustice,
Hate evil, lies, what's wrong.
What's wrong?

Now, this is the truth,
I obtained through study, work, and meditation.
As incredible as this story seems,
This stuff, and information, see?
(See The Resurrection Of Noah),

I am Jimmy, James, Jacob, Jefferson,
The information obtained on 8/4/1999,
Through vision, meditation, and the mercy of God.
I come into the physical world through
The third progression,
Like the third child, third sign (Gemini),
Third generation, Jacob,
Third president, Jefferson. Omar was third Caliph.

I am "Jewish, Christian, and Muslim," see?
And believe me, Muhammad is
The reincarnation of Moses, you see?
Obtained in a similar manner, on 5/2/2000.

And there is more, but not right now.
Please listen:
When I read Jefferson's Autobiography,
And read about the original Declaration,
Including references to slavery,
And saw the ampersands,

And read about how I (Jefferson)
Put others first, promoted and advanced them,
Explored the Northwest,
Doubled the size of the USA,
Gave it ideals,

Loved with passion,
And conviction,

Had the same personality, and character,
As I have today;

And in this life,
In my youth, was known as, "Red."

And in that (Jefferson-life) said,
The same as I say today,
The difference is ethnic background,
And better spiritual grounding, capability,
This time, you see?

So, what's up, with the Jefferson, Jacob thing?
I've had over 13 years to think about it,
Examine it, question, and confirm.
(Please read The Gospels, Daniel, Qur'an.)

So, what's up, with the Jefferson, Jacob thing?

It shows how life works, in cycles, periods, patterns,
Conforms TOTALLY with the Gospels, and Qur'an,
And of the Torah, Gospel, and Qur'an,
We are its Guardians.

Believe me, this is true.

22 WHAT TIME IS IT?

The Eight Empires
Have formed and failed,
Because they were formed with lies.

Egypt, Assyria, Babylonia, Persia, Greece, and Rome.

At home, The USA, Canada, UK, and Australia, Comprise the Seventh Power.

The Seventh creates the Eight Empire,
Including The European Union, and NATO.
But the credo is the same.

Same lies, misinformation,
Injustice forms its core,
Desolation, abomination, slavery, genocide abides.

Obscene riches for the few,
Misery for the masses.
It's good at war, imperialism, and neo-colonialism,
It's really into - Nihilism,

Creating Puppet Governments,
Fooling most of the people,
Most of the time,
Until this awesome time!

What time is it? It's Harvest Time!

What time is it? It's Harvest Time!

We all will give account, in these times.
"He" will be good and merciful to us,
For how we used our time.

23 YOU WILL NEVER FIND A GREATER LOVE

You will never find
A greater love than mine.

You can search forever and ever,
But you will never, ever
Find a greater love than mine.

You can search far and wide,
Check out all the other sides,

But you will never find
A greater love than mine.

Now that you have
The love you want,
When you want it,
How you want it,

Let us enjoy this love,
Take this gift,
Embrace this bliss,

For, love like this is
Hard to find.

Our love is
Such a special kind.

So, let us share and care.
Accept this blessing,
Take this gift,
Embrace this bliss,

For we could search forever, and ever,
Far and wide,
Check out all outer sides,
And never find a love like this.

A love like this is hard to find.
Our love is such a special kind.

And we will never, ever find
A sweeter kiss, and heaven, bliss.
We will never find a greater love,
Than this.

24 THE GUY WHO MISSED THE FLIGHT THAT CRASHED!

It's November 6, in the USA, 2004.
The Democrats are wringing their hands, lamenting,
As if they don't know about the fortunate guy
Who missed the flight that crashed!

They missed the Presidency on 9/11,
'Cause God hates devils, see?
And bad things happen, to bad people,
Can you see this, friend?

Democrats missed the chance to cleanup
Bush's mess in Iraq,
In the economy,
In just about everywhere.

But remember, the USA has had its 228 years,
To embrace what's right, live in the light;
And chose another course.

The 42 Prophet-Kings, Philosopher-Priests,
Of Matthew and of Luke, are like our own
Legitimate 42 presidents,
And then it's Harvest Time!

Bad times?
Blame bad people!

For example,
In life, if you cannot get that guy or girl,
"He" may be bad for you.
What feels good,
Is not always good for you.

If you are lucky,
You will miss the (poisoned) flight
Destined to crash!

25 YOU ARE PERFECT!

I guess all people
Are perfect in something, or other.

Michael Jordan was often
A perfect basketball player.

The '85 Chicago Bears were often perfect.
Check it out!

Did you ever see Janet Jackson
Move her hips and torso
As she sings?
She really swings:

Perfect body, perfect movement,
Perfect motion, perfect beauty.

Music is very often perfect,
And makes me feel perfectly happy.

Well, how about the perfect performance
Of this year's Boston Red Socks?

I see perfect problems, perfect solutions,
Perfect timing, every hour,

Perfect Honeys, perfect fits,
Our perfect love, that now exists,

I see perfect autumn, perfect flowers,
Love made in Heaven,
Just like ours.

You are a perfect lady,
So sexy on the outside,

Delicious on the inside,
And Heavenly too!

You are not only perfect,
But you are perfect, for me.

And I will love you with a love,
As perfect as can be.

26 YES, I LOVE YOU

This is our secret.
I love the way you look,
The thought of you,
Your voice,
The way you walk,
Your fantastic "Baby Doll,"
Your gorgeous legs,
Your lovely nose, and sexy mouth,
Your beautiful, sexy, curvy, body –
Makes me hot,
And turns me on the most,
To the utmost,
And makes me sizzle!

You're gorgeous, but
Your kind, sweet ways,
Are what I love the most.

I love to see you,
Listen to you,
Watch you move,
Move with you,
Kiss you, feel the bliss:
Your warm, sweet kiss.

I love to taste you,
Love you, completely,
Over and over!

Then, hold you in my arms,
And whisper in your ear,
This is our secret.
"Yes, I love you, my Sweet,
"Friend, and lover,
"Always, forever,
"I love you!"

27 I LOVE TO SEE YOU DANCE

I love to see your body move,
I love to see you dance,

I love to see your body move,
I love to see you groove.

I love the way you move your hips,
The way you move your torso.

You look so doggone good to me,
You are "magnifico!"

I love to see your body move,
'Cause you excite me with your groove.

I love the way you move your feet,
You look so good, it's kinda neat,

You are so sexy, when you dance.
Men come around at every chance,
To see you groove and dance.

You make me want to dance with you,
Give you a love so strong and true,

And shape our love, enhance our love,
And make our love
A groovy dance,

And make our love
A great romance!

28 ABOUT THE AUTHOR, AND OTHER BOOKS

Youssef Khalim obtained Unity in yoga on about 7/20/80. He says, "We will recombine into one faith, Judaism, Christianity, and Islam." He has been able to "see" and experience some amazing information about USA presidents Jefferson, Lincoln, and Obama; and also Prophets Moses, Muhammad, and Solomon - in visions, lucid dreams, and in meditation. Khalim makes reincarnation (resurrection) central again in our western religions. He resides in the Chicagoland area. And he is the father of Tonya, Runako, and Noah. See his books on the following websites: http://amazon.com, http://lulu.com, and http://sunracommunications.com

OTHER BOOKS

Youssef Khalim's books include *People Of The Future/Day; You Are Too Beautiful; I Love You Back; You Look So Good; The Resurrection Of Noah; Healing Begins With The Mind; Jubilee Worldwide; Lara, Forever; Tanisha Love; Galina, All About Love; Ekaterina, Hot and Lovely; Natalia, With Love; Svetlana, Angel Of Love; I Call My Sugar, Candie*; *Love of My Life;* and *The Second Coming!*

www.ingramcontent.com/pod-product-compliance
Lightning Source LLC
Chambersburg PA
CBHW041617220426
43671CB00001B/14